and the Knights
of the Round Table

empest

nd Jocelyn Potter

Pearson Education Limited
Edinburgh Gate, Harlow,
Essex CM20 2JE, England
and Associated Companies throughout the world.

ISBN: 978-1-4058-5532-7

First published by Penguin Books 2000
This edition published 2008

1 3 5 7 9 10 8 6 4 2

Text copyright © Penguin Books Ltd 2000
This edition copyright © Pearson Education Ltd 2008
Illustrations by John James

Typeset by Graphicraft Ltd, Hong Kong
Set in 11/14pt Bembo
Printed in China
SWTC/01

Published by Pearson Education Ltd in association with
Penguin Books Ltd, both companies being subsidiaries of Pearson Plc

For a complete list of the titles available in the Penguin Readers series please write to your local
Pearson Longman office or to: Penguin Readers Marketing Department, Pearson Education,
Edinburgh Gate, Harlow, Essex CM20 2JE, England.

Contents

Introduction

They went back to the place outside the church, and Sir Ector put the sword in the stone again.

'Now pull it out,' he said to Arthur.

Arthur pulled it out. It came out as easily as a knife out of butter. Sir Ector saw this and took Arthur's hand.

'You are my king,' he said.

Only the next king can pull the sword out of the stone. Many people try, but they cannot move the sword. Then young Arthur tries, and it comes out easily. Now he will be king. But will he be a good king? Will his people love him? And will his life be happy?

The story of King Arthur and the Knights of the Round Table is very, very old. People know that there was a king in Britain between the years 400 and 600. He fought the Saxons, from countries in the north of Europe, and perhaps this king was Arthur. He lived, perhaps, in Wales or in the west of England – in Somerset or Cornwall.

People wrote stories about this king hundreds of years later, but they made the stories more interesting and more exciting. At that time people were interested in magic, knights and their ladies. So people fight with swords and use magic in these stories.

Who wrote these first stories? Nobody really knows, but different people in France and Britain wrote about King Arthur and his knights. Not every book about them has the same people and stories in it. One book (1484), by Sir Thomas Malory, is very famous. He used French stories about King Arthur and wrote them in English.

Chapter 1   Arthur and Merlin

This very old story begins with Uther, a great king. He was a good man and he was king in the south of Britain. Other places were very dangerous at that time, but people did not fight in Uther's country. Uther loved a beautiful woman, Igraine, and he wanted to marry her. But she did not love him and he was very sad about that.

Merlin was a very clever man and he knew a lot of magic. He could change into an animal or bird. Sometimes, when he used magic, nobody could see him. He also helped people with his magic, and one day he came to King Uther.

'You can marry Igraine,' he said. 'I will help you. But when you have a child, you will have to give the boy to me.'

'I will give him to you,' said the King. He married Igraine and later they had a baby son. They called him Arthur. When Arthur was three days old, a very old man arrived at the door of the King's house. It was Merlin. King Uther took the child in his arms and gave him to Merlin. Merlin took the child away. He gave the boy, Arthur, to a good knight. His name was Sir ★ Ector. So Arthur lived with Sir Ector and his son, Kay, and the two boys were brothers.

◆

A short time after this happened, King Uther was very ill. He did not get better. He called for Merlin because he wanted to talk about the future of his country. Merlin came and listened to the King.

'I know that I am going to die,' King Uther said. 'Who will be king after me?'

★ Sir: a name for a knight.

1

'Call your knights and great men,' Merlin told the King. 'Tell them, "My son, Arthur, will be the next king!"'

King Uther told his people this before he died. But a lot of people wanted to be king, so the knights and great men began to fight. There was no new king for a long time.

◆

When Arthur was a young man, Merlin went to London. He visited the Archbishop, the most important man in the Church.

'Call the knights to London. Then we will find the new king,' Merlin told the Archbishop.

The knights came to London. They met at a large church, and the Archbishop spoke to them. When they came outside, they saw something strange in front of the church. It was a very large stone with a great sword in it. The sun shone on the sword and it looked very strong. The knights were excited, and started to talk about it.

'Where did it come from?'

'How did it get here?'

'Who brought the stone here? We didn't see anybody. And who put the sword in it?'

On the stone were these words:

ONLY THE KING
CAN TAKE THE SWORD FROM THE STONE

Every knight tried to pull the sword out of the stone. Nobody could do it – the sword did not come out. The knights pulled and pulled. But they could not move the sword.

'Our king is not here,' said the Archbishop. 'But I know that we will find him.'

Ten knights stayed and watched the stone. The Archbishop invited all the great men in the country to London for a big fight. There were many big fights at that time. People fought on horses with swords in their hands. The strongest and best knight always won.

'Perhaps the new king will come to the fight,' thought the Archbishop.

Sir Ector went to the fight with his two sons, Sir Kay and young Arthur. Arthur was now sixteen years old. The young men wanted to fight with the other knights, but Sir Kay did not have a sword. Arthur was a kind young man. He wanted to help.

'There is a sword in a stone outside a church. I saw it on the way here. I will get it and fight with it. Then you can have my sword,' he said to his brother.

Arthur left Sir Kay and quickly went to the church. There were no knights outside by the stone because they were at the fight. Arthur climbed down from his horse and went to the stone. He did not read the words on the stone. He took the sword in his hand and pulled. It came out of the stone easily.

He ran back to his horse with the sword. Some minutes later he met Sir Kay and Sir Ector again, and he showed them the sword.

'Where did that sword come from?' Sir Ector asked. He knew about the words on the stone.

They went back to the place outside the church, and Sir Ector put the sword in the stone again.

'Now pull it out,' he said to Arthur.

Arthur pulled it out. It came out as easily as a knife out of butter. Sir Ector saw this and took Arthur's hand.

'You are my king,' he said.

Arthur did not understand. What did his father mean?

'Arthur,' Sir Ector said slowly, 'I love you very much, but I am not really your father. Merlin, the famous man of magic, brought you to me when you were a small child. I took you into my family because he asked me. Now I know that you are the king.'

He took the sword in his hand and pulled.

'I will try to be a good king,' said Arthur. 'And I will listen to your words, because you are my father. Sir Kay, my brother, you will be an important knight and a friend to me.'

Then they went to the Archbishop and told him everything. The knights were angry. They did not think that Arthur was really the king. So the Archbishop called all the knights to the stone.

Arthur put the sword back into the stone. Every knight tried again to take it out, but it did not move. Then they watched and Arthur pulled it out easily.

Everybody shouted, 'Arthur is our king! Arthur is our king!'

◆

Many people came to see Arthur. They were all happy because now they had a kind, good king. He was strong and he was not afraid.

Merlin told Arthur the story of his parents. 'Your father was King Uther and your mother was Queen Igraine. When you were a baby, I took you to Avalon, a magic place. You were born with magic in your life. You will be the best knight and you will be the greatest king. You will live for a very long time.'

◆

So King Arthur began a new life. He took his horse and went through the country with his knights. Sometimes they had to fight bad men but they were not afraid. Arthur was a good king, and his knights were brave. His country was a quiet place again.

Chapter 2   The Round Table

King Arthur went to the north and the east with his knights and fought the Saxons. Then they came back and stopped in the town of Camelot. Arthur made it the most important town in the country. It was now his home, and the home of his brave knights.

One day King Arthur visited his friend, King Leodegraunce. He had a daughter and she was the most beautiful woman in England. The daughter's name was Guinevere. When he went back to Camelot, Arthur could not stop thinking about her.

'I love Guinevere and I want to marry her,' Arthur told Merlin. King Leodegraunce was very happy. Arthur was a good and brave man – a good husband for his lovely daughter.

So Arthur and Guinevere went to church and the Archbishop married them. Everybody enjoyed a wonderful party in Camelot.

Then Merlin made a large round table for King Arthur's knights in Camelot. There were 150 places at the great wood and stone table. King Arthur gave his best and bravest knights a place at the Round Table. Each knight had his place at the table, but no chair was better than another chair. Nobody sat at the top of a round table and nobody sat at the bottom.

'The names of the Knights of the Round Table will be famous!' cried Merlin.

◆

Some knights died and other brave and good knights came to Camelot. One day a new knight, Sir Pellinore, arrived at Camelot, and Arthur gave him a place at the Round Table.

For a long time there was one place with no knight. Merlin could see into the future.

'Only a good knight, your best knight, will sit there,' Merlin told King Arthur. 'The place is for your best knight, and he will come to it.'

After many years Sir Galahad came and sat in that place at the Round Table.

Chapter 3   The Sword, Excalibur

King Arthur went round the country on his horse. He met his people and helped them. One day he came to a great wood. When evening came, King Arthur was not out of the wood. Then he saw a very big, beautiful castle in front of him.

He went nearer, and the great door of the castle opened. A woman came out.

'King Arthur,' she said. 'I am Queen Annoure. Stay in my castle. It is getting dark. I will give you food and a bed for the night.'

Arthur was hungry and thirsty. He was also tired. He looked at the dark sky. 'Thank you,' he said, and he went in.

The Queen was kind to Arthur. She took his horse and gave it food and water. She took Arthur to the dining-room of her castle and gave him bread, meat and wine. Then one of Queen Annoure's men took the King to his bedroom, and Arthur went to sleep.

◆

The next morning, after breakfast, Queen Annoure wanted to see Arthur.

'I would like to show you my castle and the beautiful things in it,' she said. 'I am the richest person in the world. Look – everything here is mine.'

Arthur looked at her castle. They went from room to room, and each room was richer than the room before that. There were beautiful things everywhere. Queen Annoure knew a lot of magic, so she could make beautiful things.

Then they came out on to the top of the castle.

'Look at those beautiful trees and gardens,' said the Queen. 'And look at those woods. They are mine too. This is my country. And can you see that great wall round the castle? Stay with me and be king here! You cannot leave. The door of the castle is

'Stay with me and be king here!'

shut, and that great wall will stop you. My men are ready. Do not leave, or they will kill you.'

'Your magic cannot hurt me, and your men cannot kill me,' answered King Arthur.

Then, with his sword in his hand and his helmet on his head, Arthur went out of the castle, and through the door in the great wall. Nobody could stop him.

◆

Queen Annoure sent one of her men to Sir Pellinore. He lived near her castle, and he had a place at King Arthur's Round Table.

'Queen Annoure says that a very bad knight is on his way to her castle. He wants to kill her and take her money. He is very near here, and he will go past your house. Please go out and fight him for my queen,' the man said to Sir Pellinore.

So Pellinore sat on his horse and waited. He did not know that King Arthur was the 'very bad knight'. Arthur met Pellinore on the road.

'Sir! Knight!' cried Arthur. 'Why are you waiting here? Do you want to fight me?'

'Yes!' shouted Sir Pellinore, and he took his sword in his hand.

Pellinore hit the King with his sword and Arthur fell from his horse. He stood up. He was very angry and pulled out his sword. They had a long fight, and then the King's sword broke.

'Ha!' cried Sir Pellinore. 'That is the end of the fight! I can kill you now!'

Arthur threw down his sword. He ran at Sir Pellinore and threw him on to the ground. The two men were very tired, but they fought for a little longer. Then Arthur put his foot on Pellinore's head. Arthur took the helmet from his head, so Pellinore could see his face.

'Shall I kill you?' Arthur said.

Pellinore looked up and saw Arthur's face.

'My King!' he cried. 'I did not know it was you! Queen Annoure wanted me to fight a bad knight on this road.'

'I am not that bad knight! But I know you did not want to kill your king,' said King Arthur.

Then the two men were friends again.

◆

Sir Pellinore hurt King Arthur in the fight, so Merlin visited Arthur. In three days Arthur was well again.

'My sword broke in the fight,' Arthur told Merlin.

'That sword was not important,' said Merlin. 'Come with me and you will find the best sword in the world. It is a magic sword from Avalon, the place of magic.'

The King went with Merlin through a dark wood. The trees shut out the light from the sun and Arthur could not see the sky. After a long time they came to an open place in the mountains. There were no trees, but Arthur saw a strange lake. The water was very blue and there were flowers next to it.

'Now go to the lake,' Merlin told Arthur. So Arthur left his horse with Merlin and walked down to the magic lake. He looked across the quiet blue water – and there, in the centre of the lake, he suddenly saw an arm with a beautiful sword in its hand.

'Go and take it,' said Merlin. 'It is the sword Excalibur. The Lady of the Lake made it for you. She lives in her home in the water of the lake.'

A lovely young woman walked across the water and stood on the ground next to King Arthur.

'I am the Lady of the Lake. Your sword, Excalibur, is waiting for you.'

There was a boat on the water. King Arthur got into it and went to the middle of the lake. He took the sword, and the arm went into the water. When Arthur came back to Merlin, the Lady of the Lake was not there.

The sword was inside a scabbard. It was a very beautiful thing.

'That is a magic scabbard,' said Merlin. 'No man can kill a person with that scabbard. Have it with you always, because an evil woman will try to take the scabbard and the sword away from you.'

King Arthur and Merlin went home again. Arthur's knights listened happily to the stories of his journey.

Chapter 4   Morgan le Fay

Morgan le Fay was a queen, with a castle in the country of Gorres. She was a very bad woman. She could do magic, but she only used her magic for bad things. King Arthur did not know that Morgan le Fay hated him. She wanted King Arthur to die.

'She is a kind friend,' thought King Arthur. He did not know about her evil plans.

One day he went out on his horse to the woods. He wanted to catch animals, so he did not take his sword. He left Excalibur with Queen Morgan le Fay at her castle.

'I will come and get it on my way home,' he told her.

Arthur went on his horse in front of his men. He went a long way into the dark woods and then he could not find the way out again. When night came, he could not see his men anywhere.

Arthur came to a lake. Then he saw a small light on the lake and he moved nearer and nearer to it. The light was in a beautiful ship.

'I will go onto the ship,' thought Arthur.

When he was inside, he saw food and drink on the table and a bed. But he could not see anybody there.

It was late and King Arthur was tired. 'I will stay here tonight,' he thought. 'In the morning I will find my way out of the woods. Then I will get Excalibur, and go home.'

So he ate a good dinner on the ship and then he went to sleep. But when he woke up in the morning, he was not in the ship. He was in a little room with a very small window. He did not know this place. The door was shut, so he could not get out. There were three knights in the room.

'This is the castle of Sir Damas. He is a very evil knight. He caught us too, and put us here,' one of the knights told Arthur. 'Sir Damas wants us to fight for him. Then we can leave the castle. Or we will stay here and die.'

Some men came and took Arthur into a great room. Sir Damas was there.

'Will you fight for me?' Sir Damas asked.

'That is a difficult question, Sir Damas,' answered King Arthur. 'I will fight for you. But when I win, I want those three knights. Then we will all leave your castle.'

'Yes,' answered Sir Damas. 'Fight for me and you can take the three knights with you.'

'I will have to have a horse and a sword,' King Arthur said.

Then a man came into the room. He brought a sword and gave it to Arthur.

'This sword is from Queen Morgan le Fay. It is for you, King Arthur. You left it with her and she heard about your fight today. She wants you to have Excalibur,' said the man.

King Arthur looked at the sword. 'Yes, this is Excalibur,' he thought happily. No man could kill him when he had the magic scabbard.

Sir Damas gave him food and drink and he got ready for the fight.

◆

When Arthur was ready, he went outside. He saw another knight there, but he did not know him. He could not see the knight's face behind his helmet.

'Who is this knight? Which castle does he come from? Which king sent him?' thought Arthur.

The other knight also did not know King Arthur under his helmet.

The fight began. King Arthur was not happy. He could not hurt the other knight with his sword, because the sword was not Excalibur! It was a sword from Morgan le Fay's magic. It looked the same as Excalibur, but it was different. When the other knight hit Arthur with his sword, it hurt him. Arthur felt very weak.

'His sword is very strong,' thought Arthur.

King Arthur was very brave and he did not stop fighting. Many people came and watched the fight. But then Arthur's sword broke. He fell onto the ground.

'Sir!' the other knight cried. 'Say that I am the winner! Then I will not kill you!'

'No!' cried Arthur. 'I will fight – and fight.'

King Arthur took the end of his sword. He hit the knight on the head as hard as he could with it. The knight fell back and hit the ground. His sword fell from his hand, and Arthur quickly took it. When he felt the sword in his hand, he knew. It was Excalibur!

Then Arthur saw his scabbard next to the knight. He jumped up and took that too.

'Tell me – who are you? What is your name?' asked Arthur.

The knight stood up and answered, 'I am Sir Accolon, Knight of the Round Table. I am one of King Arthur's knights.'

'Tell me – why did you fight me, your king?'

'Sir, I did not know you. I came here because Queen Morgan le Fay sent me. She said to me, "King Arthur is in the castle of Sir Damas. You have to go and fight Sir Damas. Then he will not kill your king." Now I know that you are not Sir Damas. I am very sorry,' said Sir Accolon.

'And who gave you that sword?' asked Arthur.

'Queen Morgan le Fay gave it to me. She said, "Here is King Arthur's sword, Excalibur, and its scabbard. Take them for the fight. Then you will fight well and your king can leave the castle of that evil knight, Sir Damas."'

King Arthur was very angry when he heard Accolon's story.

'I know now that you did not want to kill me, Sir Accolon. You are a brave knight. Now I understand Morgan le Fay's evil plan. I had a conversation with Merlin, the man of good magic. I have to be careful with my sword and scabbard, he said. But I did not listen.'

◆

King Arthur went back to Sir Damas's castle with Sir Accolon, and they found the three knights. There was a great fight with Sir Damas, and King Arthur won with Excalibur. But after the fight he had a lot of wounds.

'Bring Sir Damas to me!' said the King.

Sir Damas came to King Arthur.

'Why did you want me to fight for you? Why did I have to fight Sir Accolon, one of my knights?' King Arthur asked him.

'Because Queen Morgan le Fay wanted it,' answered Sir Damas.

'You are not a brave man,' said Arthur, 'and now you will not be a knight. I am taking your castle from you, and everything in it. I am going to give it to your younger brother.'

Then King Arthur left. He did not go to Camelot because he wanted to get well first.

◆

Morgan le Fay went to stay at Camelot, and King Arthur was not there.

'King Arthur is dead now!' she thought. But then her men came to Camelot, and they told her about the fight.

'King Arthur did not die in the fight,' they said.

Morgan le Fay went to Queen Guinevere and said, 'I have to go back to my country now. My people want me there.'

Queen Guinevere knew nothing about Morgan le Fay's magic and her evil ideas.

'Don't go,' she answered. 'The King is coming back to Camelot. I think he will be here tomorrow or the next day. He will be happy when he sees you.'

'No! No!' said Morgan le Fay. 'I cannot stay – I have to go.'

And so she left Camelot on her black horse.

◆

Morgan le Fay and her black horse did not stop that day or that night. When she met people on her journey, she asked them: 'Where is King Arthur? Tell me, where is the King?'

After a long time she heard about him.

'The King is ill,' a man told her. 'He fought a knight at Sir Damas's castle. The knight wounded King Arthur, so he cannot go back to Camelot. He is staying with the nuns. They are good women, and he will get better there with their help.'

The nuns worked for the church and helped people. They were very kind and lived in a large, quiet house. People could stay there when they wanted their help.

Morgan le Fay said thank you to the man and went to visit the nuns.

'I am on a long journey, and I am hungry and thirsty,' she said. 'Please can I eat something?'

The nuns brought food and drink and gave it to Morgan le Fay.

'Is there another visitor here?' she asked.

'Yes,' the nuns said. 'King Arthur is here. A knight's sword wounded him in a fight. He will leave when his wounds are better. He is sleeping. You can speak to him when he wakes up.'

'Oh! The King!' Morgan le Fay cried. 'I cannot wait because I have to go home. But please, can I look at him? I love our king and I would like to see him!'

'We cannot wake up the King! He is in his bed and he is ill,' said one of the nuns.

'Please, let me sit next to him for a minute or two. I want to see his face!' asked Morgan le Fay again.

The nun thought about it. 'Yes, all right. You can go and look at him. But do not make any noise. Do not wake him up.'

Morgan le Fay went into King Arthur's room. She stood next to him and watched him. The King was asleep, but he had his hand on Excalibur. She could not take the sword away because she did not want to wake him. Then she saw the scabbard at the end of the bed. Quickly she took it and put it under her clothes. Nobody could see it there. She went out of the room and said thank you and goodbye to the nuns. Then Morgan le Fay got on her black horse and left.

◆

Later, when King Arthur opened his eyes, he could not see the scabbard.

'Something is wrong,' he thought. 'Where is the scabbard of my sword, Excalibur?'

He was very angry and called a nun. 'Did anybody come into this room when I was asleep?' he asked her.

'Queen Morgan le Fay came,' she said. 'But no other person. She could not stay, but she came into the room. She loves you and she wanted to see your face.'

'Thank you,' said the King. 'Thank you for your help. I came here to your house when I was ill. You were kind and good to me. My wounds are getting better. But I have to go now – it is important! I have to follow Queen Morgan le Fay. When she visited me in my room, she took the scabbard of my sword, Excalibur.'

The nuns did not want him to leave because he was not ready. But they helped him onto his horse, and he left their house.

◆

King Arthur did not stop for hours. Then he came to a river. There was a man there with his animals.

'Did anybody come this way?' asked the King.

'Yes,' answered the man. 'A beautiful woman came on a black horse. She went across the river here very quickly and did not stop.'

King Arthur went over the river, through woods and up a mountain. Then he looked down, and he saw Morgan le Fay a long way away.

Morgan le Fay looked back and she saw the King. The ground was hard and there were a lot of stones. She went across the stones and arrived at a lake. The lake was black. No animal drank the water. No birds sang in the trees.

Queen Morgan le Fay got off her black horse and took out the scabbard of King Arthur's sword, Excalibur. She threw it into the water.

'King Arthur will never have it!' she cried. 'That scabbard will not help him now when men fight him. Nobody will find it here – at the bottom of this lake!'

Then she quickly went away on her horse, back to her castle.

King Arthur followed Morgan le Fay and came to the same place. He could not see the Queen.

'Which way did she go?' King Arthur thought. 'Where did the horse go? I cannot follow the horse's feet across these stones.' King Arthur looked and looked. He saw nothing, so he went home to Camelot without his scabbard.

King Arthur had Excalibur. But because of the evil Queen, he did not have the magic scabbard. It stayed at the bottom of the black lake and he never found it.

Chapter 5   Vivien and Merlin

When King Arthur was a young man, Merlin, the man of magic, helped him in every way. He taught him to be a good king and a brave knight. Merlin helped Arthur to be kind to everybody in his country, so they all loved him. With Merlin's help, Arthur built the beautiful city, Camelot. Camelot had roads and houses and a great castle.

Later, when Merlin was an old man, he came to King Arthur again.

'I have to say goodbye now,' said Merlin.

'Goodbye? Why, Merlin?' asked King Arthur.

'I am going to die,' Merlin told him. 'I will not always be here. In the future, when you make mistakes, my magic will not help you.'

'Oh Merlin!' said King Arthur sadly. 'I do not want you to go!'

'I am going down into a dark cave, and I cannot come back from that cave.'

'But Merlin,' King Arthur cried, 'you know a lot of magic. Can you not stop this? Do you have to die?'

'I cannot stop it,' answered Merlin. 'You have to be a strong king without me now!'

◆

After Merlin spoke to King Arthur, Lady Vivien came to Camelot. Before this time, she lived with the Lady of the Lake. The Lady of the Lake made Excalibur and she knew a lot of magic.

Vivien learned magic from the Lady of the Lake. Then she went to Camelot and studied with Merlin. When she knew all Merlin's magic, she thought, 'He is an old man. I cannot kill him because his magic is strong. But I can send him away somewhere so he cannot come back. Then I will have the greatest and strongest magic in the world.'

Vivien went on a long journey with Merlin to another country. They climbed a high grey mountain and came to a dark place with a lot of trees and a small river. There they saw a magic cave inside the mountain.

'The mouth of the cave is open now,' said Merlin to Vivien. 'When you say the magic words, the mouth of the cave will shut.'

'I know these magic words. But which words will open it again?' asked Vivien.

'I do not know,' said Merlin.

'I want to look inside the cave,' Vivien said. 'Please come with me. Show me the way.'

So Merlin went into the cave first, but Vivien ran out quickly. She shouted the magic words, and the mouth of the cave shut loudly. Merlin was inside and could not get out.

Some people say that the great Merlin is there now, inside the cave. One day, they say, somebody will break open the big stone door of the cave. Then Merlin will come out again and help the world with his magic. He will, they say, teach everybody to be good and happy.

But after that sad day, King Arthur had no help from his friend, Merlin.

Chapter 6　Sir Meligrance

It was the month of May. The weather was warm and the sky was blue. The flowers looked very beautiful in the sun.

Queen Guinevere called her ten knights and her ladies and said, 'Let's enjoy this beautiful day. We can look for some lovely spring flowers. Let's take some food and drink and have a party in the wood.'

So Guinevere left the castle with her knights and her ladies. Some boys from the castle went with them and carried their things.

So Merlin went into the cave first.

All day they enjoyed the sun. In the afternoon they sat under the tall green trees. They ate and they talked. Then evening came.

'Now let's go home,' the Queen said. 'King Arthur is waiting for us at Camelot.'

They were all ready when suddenly twenty men with swords and helmets jumped out from the trees.

'Stand there and do not move!' one of the men shouted. 'Or we will kill you all!'

It was Sir Meligrance, with his men. He loved Queen Guinevere and he wanted to take her to his castle.

'I love you,' he said, 'and you are here without the King!'

'Sir Meligrance,' cried the Queen. 'King Arthur made you a Knight of the Round Table! A knight has to be a good man. How can you take away your king's wife?'

'I only know that I love you. My men will help me. They will fight your knights,' answered Sir Meligrance.

Guinevere's ten knights turned to Sir Meligrance.

'We will not stand here when you take our queen away, Sir! We will stop you.'

Sir Meligrance and his men had better swords and helmets than Guinevere's knights. His men were ready – Guinevere's men were only there for the flowers.

The fight began. Guinevere's knights were brave and fought hard. But they could not win. Sir Meligrance's men were too strong for them. And there were twenty of them. They wounded all Guinevere's good knights in the fight.

'Stop!' cried Guinevere to her knights. 'Or they will kill you.' She looked at Sir Meligrance. 'All right, Sir Meligrance. I will come with you.'

She was very angry and afraid. 'Come with me, my brave knights, to Sir Meligrance's castle.'

So Queen Guinevere and her people went to the castle, but first the Queen spoke to one of the boys.

21

'You have a good, fast horse,' she said to him quietly. 'Go quickly to Camelot! Tell the King and Sir Lancelot!'

Sir Meligrance saw the boy when he left, but his men could not catch him.

◆

The boy arrived at Camelot and saw Sir Lancelot. Sir Lancelot was the strongest of King Arthur's knights. When he heard the story, Lancelot quickly put his helmet on his head and took his sword.

'I will go now to Sir Meligrance's castle and find the Queen,' said Sir Lancelot to the boy. 'Go and tell the King.'

When Lancelot came near the castle, he thought, 'Sir Meligrance's men will wait next to the road. They will come out when I go past. So I will not take the road – I will go through the wood.'

Lancelot was right. Sir Meligrance's men waited by the road, but they did not see the knight.

Sir Meligrance saw Lancelot outside the castle. His men were by the road, and suddenly he was afraid. Lancelot was brave and strong. He could fight Sir Meligrance and win.

So Sir Meligrance went to Queen Guinevere and said, 'Oh, my Queen, I am sorry! Please say you are not angry with me. I will take you back to Camelot and I will fight for King Arthur. I want to be a good knight.'

The Queen did not know about Lancelot and Sir Meligrance's men, so she answered, 'Yes, you are sorry. I can see that. I will not be angry with you.'

◆

When Lancelot arrived at the castle, Guinevere told him, 'I am not angry with Meligrance now. Let's stay here tonight and we will go back to Camelot tomorrow morning.'

Sir Lancelot was very angry and Sir Meligrance knew it. 'Sir Lancelot will kill me when the Queen leaves this castle,' he thought.

They ate in the castle's great dining-room. When they finished dinner, Sir Meligrance said to Lancelot, 'I will take you to your room and you can sleep.'

He showed Lancelot into a room with a door in the floor. Sir Lancelot put his foot on the door and it opened. He fell into a little room below the door and he could not climb up again.

Sir Meligrance went to the Queen.

'Sir Lancelot did not want to stay here. He went back to Camelot,' he told her.

◆

The next day Queen Guinevere went back to Camelot with Sir Meligrance. When they arrived, they saw King Arthur.

'Your knights are saying that Sir Meligrance took you away to his castle,' said King Arthur.

'Yes,' Queen Guinevere told King Arthur. 'Meligrance took me to his castle and my knights fought for me. But Meligrance had a lot of men and they were too strong for us. But he is sorry, so I am not angry with him now.'

'Tell me, Sir Meligrance,' Arthur asked. 'Are the Queen's knights right? What happened when you met Queen Guinevere in the wood with her knights and ladies?'

Sir Meligrance answered, 'I did not take the Queen away, King Arthur. She came with me because she loves me.'

The King was very angry with Sir Meligrance.

◆

A girl in Sir Meligrance's castle carried food to Sir Lancelot every day. She liked him, because he was strong and brave. So when Sir Meligrance took Guinevere to Camelot, the girl opened the door in the floor. Sir Lancelot left the room and went quickly back to King Arthur's castle.

The King was with the Queen and his knights in the great dining-room when Sir Lancelot came in. He saw Sir Meligrance there and was angry. He looked at Sir Meligrance.

'You took away Queen Guinevere to your castle,' cried Sir Lancelot. 'She is not angry with you now, so I will not kill you for that. But now you say that she loves you. For this I will kill you! I am the strongest of King Arthur's knights, so I will fight you without a helmet. But I will win!'

Sir Meligrance quickly moved closer to Sir Lancelot. He hit the other knight's head with his sword because he had no helmet. But Lancelot jumped away and cut Sir Meligrance's helmet in two. And Sir Meligrance fell to the ground – dead.

Chapter 7   Sir Tristram

One day the King of Lyonesse went into the woods because he wanted to catch animals. He made a long journey and at the end of the day he could not find the road home. His queen waited in their castle, but he did not come back.

'Where is the King?' she thought. 'He knows that I am going to have a child.'

So the Queen went out into the woods and looked for the King. She walked a long way and began to feel very tired. In the evening she slept under a tree. There her baby boy was born.

'I am going to die,' she thought. 'I am very ill.' She took the baby in her arms.

'Oh, my little son,' cried the Queen. 'I will give you the name Tristram. It means "sad", and I am sad. I know I am not going to live. But you, my dear child, will be a brave knight when you are a man.'

The King found a way back to his castle, but the Queen was not there. His men went into the woods and looked for her.

They found the Queen and the child under a tree and took them back to the castle. The Queen told the King the baby's name – and then she died.

For many days the King did not speak or eat. 'He will die too,' people said, 'and the little boy Tristram will be our king.' But after a long time the King began to enjoy life again.

◆

Seven years later the King of Lyonesse married again, and the new queen had a son. She loved her son very much, but she did not like Tristram, the son of her husband's first wife.

One day the Queen thought of a plan. She made a drink for Tristram and put some poison in it.

'He will think it is wine,' she thought. 'But when he drinks it, he will die.' She put the glass on the table, ready for Tristram. 'Everything is ready,' she thought. 'Good!'

But the Queen's son came into the room before Tristram. He was very thirsty and he drank from the glass. Then he fell on the floor and died.

The Queen tried to kill Tristram a second time. Again she put some poison into his drink. She put the glass on the table and again waited for Tristram. This time the King came into the room. He put his hand out to the glass of wine, but the Queen cried, 'Do not drink it!'

The King suddenly remembered his second son. There was poison in his drink! Then he understood the Queen's evil plan.

'You wanted to kill Tristram, but your son drank the poison! So you tried to kill Tristram again, but I nearly drank it!' The King was very angry. 'Make a fire! Take the Queen and put her in it!' he shouted to his men.

But when the fire was ready, Tristram came to his father. He fell down at his father's feet.

'Father, do not do this! Take your wife back. Love her, and she will love you. She hates me – so send me away. Then you will be happy again.'

So Tristram went to live with his father's brother, Mark. Mark was King of Cornwall. He loved Tristram and Tristram loved his uncle. He was happy there. When he arrived there, Tristram was a boy. Some years later, he was a strong, brave man.

◆

The King of Ireland also had a son, Sir Marhaus. Nobody could fight him and win. One day, Sir Marhaus came across the sea to King Mark's castle.

'I am the best and strongest knight in Ireland! Send a knight to me and I will fight him. Then you will see!'

Not one of King Mark's knights wanted to fight Sir Marhaus.

Then Tristram went to his uncle and said, 'I am not a boy now – I am a man. Make me a knight and send me. I can fight Sir Marhaus and win.'

King Mark thought for a long time. 'I do not want to send you, but the other knights will not fight him,' he said.

So the King made his brother's son, Tristram, a knight and Tristram got ready for the fight.

Many people came and watched the two men. They fought with their swords all day. Sir Marhaus was strong, but he was older than Sir Tristram. He was not as quick on his feet. He could not hit Tristram.

The sun was hot, and Sir Marhaus started to feel tired. Tristram's sword cut through Sir Marhaus's helmet and killed him. His men took the dead man away to his ship.

Sir Marhaus also wounded Tristram badly in the fight, and the young man was very ill. There was poison in the wound.

Nobody could make Sir Tristram's wound better. After some time, an old woman came and looked at it.

She said, 'Ah! The poison in this wound came from Ireland. Send your knight there and somebody will make him better.'

◆

So King Mark sent Sir Tristram in a ship to Ireland. Sir Tristram used another name because he killed the son of the King of Ireland.

On the ship Sir Tristram looked out at the green sea water. Birds flew in the sky. He took his harp and began to play a song. He played the harp very beautifully. When his ship came near Ireland, the King heard the sound of the music. He asked Tristram to his castle, because he wanted his daughter to play the harp.

'Where did you get that wound?' the King of Ireland asked.

'Some bad men fought me on my journey,' said Tristram. He could not tell the King about his fight with Sir Marhaus.

'I will ask my daughter, Isolt, to make your wound better. Then will you teach her to play the harp?'

'Yes, Sir,' said Tristram.

The King told his daughter about his idea.

'I will be a good student, Father,' said Isolt.

She carefully cleaned the wound and stayed near Tristram's bed for many days and nights. Then, when he was well again, Tristram taught Isolt the harp. She enjoyed playing it and learned well. They were very happy. Tristram liked Isolt very much and she liked him too.

◆

Isolt knew another knight. His name was Sir Palamides. He loved Isolt and wanted to marry her. He asked her again and again. She did not like him, but he did not listen to her.

One day there was a big fight between the great men and knights in the country. A lot of people watched these fights. The knights were on the horses, with swords in their hands.

Sir Palamides wanted to fight. He had a black helmet and black clothes, and he sat on a black horse. Tristram had a white helmet, white clothes and a white horse. The two knights began to fight. Sir Tristram moved quickly and hit Sir Palamides with his sword. The black knight fell off his horse onto the ground. Then Tristram stood over him with his sword.

'Leave here! Do not speak to Isolt again — or I will kill you!' he cried.

◆

After the fight, Sir Tristram went back to Cornwall. He told his uncle about Isolt.

'So Isolt is beautiful and kind? I can marry Isolt, and then the King of Ireland and I will be friends. It will be good for our two countries,' King Mark said. 'Ask the King of Ireland for me'

So Tristram went back to Ireland.

'King Mark wants to marry. Will you give him your lovely daughter, Isolt? He is a good man and he will love her,' Tristram said to the King of Ireland.

'Yes, it will be a good thing for this country and for Cornwall,' answered the King of Ireland. And he sent Isolt to King Mark.

Tristram took Isolt on his ship. He played beautiful songs on his harp for her. Tristram loved Isolt and she loved him.

'I cannot marry you because you are going to marry King Mark. But he is a good man and he will love you well,' said Tristram.

After many days at sea, the ship came to Cornwall.

'I have to leave you now, dear Isolt,' Tristram said sadly. 'I am going away to Camelot. I want to be a Knight of the Round Table. I will fight for King Arthur. But please remember this — I am your friend and I will always love you. When you want my help, I will come.'

◆

So Isolt married King Mark, and he gave her many lovely things. But one day Sir Palamides suddenly arrived and carried Isolt away on his horse.

Another knight went after him, and Sir Palamides fought him. Isolt ran away. She ran and ran through the wood.

'Night is coming,' thought Isolt. 'Nobody will find me here in the dark wood.' She sat down and cried. Then she saw a lake.

'I will jump into the water and die! Then that evil Sir Palamides cannot hurt me or take me away.'

Isolt stood by the lake and looked into the cold water.

She heard the sound of a horse and turned round. It was not Sir Palamides. It was another knight.

'Who are you?' asked Isolt. She was afraid.

'I am Sir Atherp,' answered the knight. 'Why are you here in the wood at night, Queen Isolt? Do not be afraid. I will not hurt you. I hope I can help you.'

'I ran away from Sir Palamides. He wants to take me away! Oh, please help me!'

'It is dangerous for you here,' Sir Atherp said. 'Come with me to my castle.'

Later that night, Sir Palamides arrived at the castle of Sir Atherp.

'Open the doors!' he shouted, but nobody answered.

◆

Sir Tristram was on his way to Camelot when a man ran to him.

'Sir Palamides took Isolt away,' he said.

Tristram was very angry. He went back to Cornwall quickly and looked for Isolt. He saw a knight on the ground in a wood.

'Sir Palamides wounded me in a fight,' said the man. Tristram gave the brave knight a drink of water.

'Where did Isolt go?' Sir Tristram asked the knight.

'I do not know,' answered the knight. 'She ran away when she saw the fight.'

'I have to find her,' said Sir Tristram, and he jumped back on his horse. He came to a lake and looked at the ground.

'Isolt was here,' he thought. 'And another person on a horse. I will follow them!'

After a short time he came to a castle. Outside the castle was Sir Palamides.

Sir Palamides saw Sir Tristram and fought him. But Sir Tristram was stronger. Tristram threw Palamides off his horse and the evil knight fell onto the ground. Sir Palamides stood up and pulled his sword out of its scabbard. Then Tristram got off his horse and took out his sword. The two men fought there in front of the castle.

Isolt was inside the castle. She heard the noise of the fight, and looked down from her window.

'Tristram is here!' she cried. 'He will help me!'

She watched the fight. Palamides fell again and Tristram stood over him with his sword.

'No,' shouted Isolt loudly. 'Do not kill him!' Sir Atherp's men opened the castle doors and Isolt ran outside. 'Please do not kill him, kind Sir Tristram. He fought bravely. Send him to King Arthur and he will learn to be a good knight. Then he can fight for the King.'

'I will do this for you,' answered Tristram.

So Sir Palamides went to Camelot and learned to be a very good knight.

◆

Sir Tristram took Isolt to King Mark, and he stayed in Cornwall with them. But the King began to be afraid of him.

'Sir Tristram is young and brave,' he thought. 'He fought Sir Palamides for my queen, Isolt. Perhaps now she will love Tristram, and will not love me.'

One day Tristram went with Isolt to the beach. King Mark followed them there and watched them. Tristram played a beautiful song for Isolt on his harp. She listened with a smile on her face.

Suddenly King Mark came with his sword.

'Why are you singing love songs to my wife?' he shouted. 'I am going to kill you for this!' Tristram had no sword and could not stop King Mark. The King wounded Tristram very badly and he fell at Isolt's feet and died.

Day after day, Isolt sat and looked at the sea. She did not eat or drink. She did not speak to anybody again. She cried because Tristram was dead. Then she died too.

◆

When King Arthur heard the story of Tristram and Isolt, he was very sorry. Tristram was a brave Knight of the Round Table. Arthur was very angry with King Mark, so he sent another knight to Cornwall. That knight killed him.

Chapter 8   The Grail

King Arthur and his Knights of the Round Table were in Camelot. One day an old man with white hair and in white clothes came to the King.

'My King, I am bringing you a young knight. He is the son of a great man and he will do great things.'

The King saw a young man. He wore red clothes and a red helmet and his face was very beautiful.

For a long time there was one place at the Round Table without a knight at it. Years before, Merlin said, 'Only a good knight, your best knight, will sit there. The place is for your best knight, and he will come to it.'

This was the only place with no name on it. The old man took the young knight to that place at the Round Table. There was a name there for the first time. It said, in gold letters: SIR GALAHAD.

'Sit here,' said the old man. Then he left King Arthur and the Knights of the Round Table and nobody saw him again.

'Who is this young man? Why is he sitting there? Why is he not afraid?' asked the King. 'Does anybody know him?'

'I know him,' said Sir Lancelot. 'When I was on a journey, a nun came outside with this young man. She brought him to me and said, "His name is Galahad. He has to be a knight. It is very important." Then she took him inside again.'

The other knights looked at Galahad and they looked at Sir Lancelot. Their two faces were nearly the same.

'Sir Lancelot married when he was very young,' remembered one of the knights. 'This is Sir Lancelot's son.'

Sir Lancelot smiled at his son but said nothing.

King Arthur made Galahad a knight and they all sat down at the Round Table. Suddenly they heard a loud noise. Then there was a great white light.

They looked up and saw a gold cup above the table. What was it? Where did it come from? And then suddenly it was not there!

Nobody spoke. Then Sir Galahad said, 'That is the Grail*, and it is in this country! I will go out and look for it. I will come back when I find it.'

'We will go with you,' said Sir Lancelot, Sir Bors and Sir Percivale.

King Arthur was very sad. He looked round the Round Table at his knights. Then he spoke to them.

'We were brothers, but this will be the end of our Round Table. You are leaving and I will not see you again.'

The four knights got on their horses and left Camelot. For many years they looked for the Grail but they found nothing.

Other knights also left and looked for the Grail. Nobody found it and some knights never came back to Camelot. The Round Table was different now, and King Arthur was very sad.

◆

* The Grail: A gold cup. Jesus used it before he died.

They looked up and saw a gold cup above the table.

After many years Sir Galahad, Sir Percivale and Sir Bors came to a place near the sea. They looked down and saw a ship. It was evening, but white light shone from the ship.

'I know that we are going to find the Grail,' said Sir Galahad.

They went down to the sea and onto the ship. There, on a table, was the Grail. They were all very excited.

'Look!' cried Sir Galahad. 'Here is the Grail! Now we can end our journey.'

The knights were all very tired and they fell asleep. The ship went out to sea. The next morning, when the knights woke up, they were near a great city.

'We have to take the Grail into the city,' said Sir Galahad. So they took the Grail and left the ship.

◆

There was no king in that country, because the dead king had no son. The great men sat in the castle and thought about the problem.

When King Arthur's knights arrived at the castle with the Grail, everybody was excited. Then an old man came into the castle. He had white clothes and white hair. The knights knew him when they saw him.

'These three knights are here at the end of a long journey,' said the old man, 'and they have the Grail. Take the youngest knight, a very brave man, and make him your king.'

Then the old man left. Nobody saw him come and nobody saw him go. So Sir Galahad was now the new king.

'I found the Grail and I am happy now,' Sir Galahad said. He built a beautiful church and put the Grail in it.

Then the old man came to him again.

'Your work is done. Now you are going to die,' he said.

Sir Galahad was not afraid. In the morning they found him dead in front of the Grail. And his face was very happy.

◆

Sir Bors went back to Camelot.

'We found the Grail and do not have to look for it now,' he told King Arthur.

Many other knights also came back and sat at the Round Table again. King Arthur was happy – but he was also sad.

'I know that the end of the Round Table is coming. Many brave knights are dead. And no new knights will come and take their places,' King Arthur said sadly.

Chapter 9   King Arthur Dies

One day, King Arthur and Sir Gawain, one of his best knights, went to France. Sir Lancelot was in France at the time, and King Arthur was angry with him. He wanted to fight him there.

When Arthur was away, the evil knight Sir Mordred came to Camelot. He wanted to take Queen Guinevere away.

'King Arthur is dead!' he told the Queen. 'He died in France in a fight. I am now king, and you will be my queen.'

'I will die first!' cried the Queen.

Guinevere ran away to a castle in London, and her knights went with her. Mordred came to London with his men. But the walls of the castle were very strong, and he could not get inside.

Then one of Mordred's men came to him and said, 'King Arthur is coming back to England with his men and a lot of ships.'

Mordred went to Dover with his men and waited for King Arthur. There was a great fight, but Sir Mordred's men could not win. They ran away.

But one of Sir Mordred's men wounded Sir Gawain, and King Arthur found the brave knight on the ground.

'I am dying. Give me a pen and paper. I want to write to Sir Lancelot.'

He wrote:

To Lancelot,

I know that I am dying. You are my brother and I love you. Please come and help King Arthur in his fight with evil Sir Mordred. No knight is braver than you.

Goodbye, my friend!

Gawain

And then he died. King Arthur was very sad because he loved Gawain very much. He sat on the ground next to the dead knight and cried all night.

◆

Sir Mordred found more men and they waited for Arthur at a place near a lake. King Arthur knew the place – Excalibur came from the same lake.

On the night before the fight, Arthur saw Sir Gawain in his sleep. Gawain spoke to him.

'Do not fight Mordred now. In one month Lancelot will come with his men. He will help you and then the Queen can go back to Camelot.'

The King called his knights and told them about Sir Gawain.

'We will not fight today. I will go and speak with Mordred. Come with me and bring your swords. But leave them in their scabbards. Take them out only when Mordred or his knights take out theirs. Then kill them!'

King Arthur sent a man to Mordred. The man told him about Arthur's plan. There was no fight that day. Then Arthur met Mordred. The two men stood and talked. The King's knights stood near the King, and Mordred's knights stood near Mordred.

Suddenly something jumped on the foot of one of Mordred's knights. He pulled out his sword and killed the animal.

The other knights saw his sword and took out their swords.

'This is an unhappy day!' cried King Arthur and they began to fight.

They fought all day. When evening came, King Arthur saw only two of his knights, Sir Lucan and Sir Bedivere. His other knights were dead. Arthur cried when he saw his brave knights on the ground.

Mordred stood with his sword and looked at his dead men on the ground. Then Arthur ran to Mordred and killed him. Mordred fell, but he wounded King Arthur with his sword.

Sir Lucan and Sir Bedivere took the King to a little church near the lake. But after they arrived, Sir Lucan also died of his wounds.

The sky was dark and it was a cold night. Arthur felt very weak.

'I am also going to die now. It is time. Please take my sword, Excalibur. Go to the lake and throw it into the water,' he told Sir Bedivere.

Sir Bedivere took the sword and walked to the lake. Then he looked at the beautiful sword.

'Why do I have to throw this beautiful sword into the lake? That will not help King Arthur,' he thought.

So he put Excalibur under a big stone, and went back to the King. He said, 'I did it. I threw your sword into the lake.'

'What did you see there?' the King asked. He was very cold and his wounds hurt him.

'I saw the water, the sky and the stones. That is all.'

'Then you did not do the right thing. You did not throw the sword into the lake,' King Arthur said. 'Go again, and throw Excalibur into the water. Then come to me again.'

Sir Bedivere went again to the lake and took the sword from under the stone. He looked again at the beautiful sword and thought, 'I cannot throw this sword into the water. I want to have

An arm came up out of the water and caught the sword.

it. Then I will always remember King Arthur.'

So again he put the sword under a stone and again he went back to King Arthur.

'I saw the water, the sky and the stones. Then the sword fell into the lake,' he said.

'Go again,' the King said very sadly. 'Go quickly, because I am dying.'

'Oh my King! I am very sorry,' said Bedivere. 'I will do it now.'

He went back to the lake very quickly and got Excalibur. This time he threw it hard over the water. An arm came up out of the water and caught the sword. Then the arm took it down into the lake.

Sir Bedivere went back and told the King about the arm.

'Now,' said King Arthur, 'take me to the lake quickly.'

Sir Bedivere carried the King to the lake. There was a long black boat on the water and some ladies in black dresses were in the boat. The Lady of the Lake and Queen Morgan le Fay were two of the ladies.

He looked at their faces and thought, 'I know these faces. I knew these ladies when they lived. Now they are dead, but I remember them.'

'Please put me on the boat now,' said King Arthur. So Sir Bedivere put him on the boat and the ladies stood round him.

'I am leaving you now, and I want you to tell the story of King Arthur and the Knights of the Round Table. I will come again one day when my country asks for me,' called King Arthur to Sir Bedivere from the boat.

Those were the King's last words. The boat went out across the water. Sir Bedivere stood and cried.

And that is the end of the story of King Arthur and his brave Knights of the Round Table.

ACTIVITIES

Chapters 1–2

Before you read

1 What do you know about King Arthur and the Knights of the Round Table? Discuss this and then read the Introduction to the book.

2 Look at the Word List at the back of the book. Find new words in your dictionary.

   a Are knights in stories usually *brave* or *evil*?

   b Do they carry *stones* or *swords*?

   c Do they wear *harps* or *helmets*?

   d Do they work for *kings* and *queens* or for *nuns*?

   e Do they stay in *castles* or in *caves*?

While you read

3 Write the names.

   a King .... and Queen .... are Arthur's parents.

   b .... takes Arthur away when he is a baby.

   c Arthur thinks that .... is his father.

   d He thinks that .... is his brother.

4 Which are the right words in these sentences?

   a When Uther dies, England *has / does not have* a new king.

   b Arthur takes the sword from the stone *after a long time / easily*.

   c Arthur marries *Guinevere / Leodegrance* in Camelot.

   d *Some knights are / No knight is* more important than other knights at King Arthur's Round Table.

   e The empty chair at the Round Table is for *Sir Pellimore / Sir Galahad*.

After you read

5 Work with another student. Have this conversation.

   Student A: You are Merlin. What happened to Arthur after he was born? Why? Tell him.

   Student B: You are Arthur. Ask Merlin questions.

Chapter 3

Before you read

6 Discuss these questions. What do you think?

    a Chapter 3 is about a sword, Excalibur. How will it be different from other swords?

    b Look at the picture on page 8. Arthur and a rich queen are standing on her castle. Will Arthur stay there with her? Why (not)?

While you read

7 Answer Yes or No to these questions.

    a Does Arthur want to be king in Queen Annoure's country?   .....

    b Can Queen Annoure's magic hurt Arthur?   .....

    c Does Sir Pellinore know that he is fighting his king?   .....

    d Does Arthur's sword break in the fight?   .....

8 What happens first? Number the sentences, 1–6.

    a Arthur and Merlin go back to Camelot with the sword.   .....

    b Arthur takes a boat and gets the sword.   .....

    c Merlin helps Arthur after the fight.   .....

    d Merlin takes Arthur to a strange lake.   .....

    e The Lady of the Lake says that Arthur's sword is waiting for him.   .....

    f There is a beautiful sword in the middle of the lake.   .....

After you read

9 Work with another student. Have this conversation.

    Student A: You are one of Queen Annoure's men. You watched the fight between King Arthur and Sir Pellinore. Now you are in the castle. Answer the Queen's questions.

    Student B: You are Queen Annoure. You want to know about the fight. Ask questions.

Chapter 4

Before you read

10 Merlin said, 'An evil woman will try to take the scabbard and the sword away from you. What will she do?' Discuss your ideas.

While you read

11 Write one word in each sentence.

Morgan le Fay .... King Arthur, but he doesn't know that. He leaves .... with her at her castle. After a night on a ship, he wakes up in the castle of Sir .... Arthur fights another knight, but his .... breaks. .... Morgan le Fay gave Excalibur to the other knight. Arthur then fights Sir Damas and takes away his .... But when Arthur is staying with some ...., Morgan le Fay visits them.

12 Finish the sentences with words on the right.

a	Morgan le Fay finds King Arthur	his scabbard into a lake.
b	She takes his	before he is well.
c	Arthur leaves the nuns' house	his scabbard again.
d	He follows Morgan le Fay	in the nuns' house.
e	Morgan le Fay throws	scabbard from his bed.
f	Arthur never sees	for hours.

After you read

13 Discuss these questions.

    a How does Arthur feel when he gets back to Camelot at the end of this chapter?

    b How does Morgan le Fay feel after she throws the sword into the lake?

    c Why is Arthur a weaker king at the end of this story?

Chapters 5–6

Before you read

14 Talk to another student. How important is Merlin to King Arthur? Can Arthur be king without him? Why (not)?

While you read

15 Who:

    a is going to die in a dark cave? ....

    b wants to have the strongest magic in the
world? ....

    c has no more help from Merlin? ....

16 Are these sentences right (✓) or wrong (✗)?

    a Queen Guinevere loves Sir Meligrance. .....

    b Guinevere's knights fight for her. .....

    c Meligrance knows that Sir Lancelot is stronger than him. .....

    d Arthur is very angry with Guinevere. .....

    e Lancelot kills Meligrance. .....

After you read

17 Discuss these questions.

    a When Merlin goes into the cave with Vivien, does he know about her plans?

    b How does Meligrance catch Lancelot? How does Lancelot get away?

Chapter 7

Before you read

18 In the story of Tristram and Isolt, Tristram and his uncle love the same woman. What will happen, do you think? Think of a possible story and tell other students.

While you read

19 Who are these sentences about? Write *Sir T* for Sir Tristram, *Sir M* for Sir Marhaus or *Sir P* for Sir Palamides.

    a The Queen tries to kill him with poison. ....

    b He is the strongest knight in Ireland. ....

    c He is Isolt's brother. ....

    d He wears black and has a black horse. ....

    e He takes Isolt away from her husband. ....

    f He learns to be a good knight in Camelot. ....

    g He dies at Isolt's feet. ....

After you read

20 What can you say to these people? Find a sentence.

'*You* marry her!'   'Stay at home!'   'Take your sword!'

'Find a different girl!'   'Don't drink it!'

  a The Queen is going to have a baby and she goes into the woods without any knights.

  b The Queen's son is going to drink a glass of wine. There is poison in it.

  c Sir Palamides doesn't listen when Isolt says no to him.

  d Tristram takes Isolt to Cornwall.

  e Tristram goes to the beach with Isolt and his harp.

21 Work with another student. Think of a happier end to the story of Tristram and Isolt.

Chapters 8–9

Before you read

22 Look at the picture on page 33. Find the Grail in the picture. What is it? Why is it important? Do you know?

23 What did Merlin say about Sir Galahad in Chapter 2 of this book? Can you remember? Look on page 6.

While you read

24 Put the right words in the sentences.

church   father   knights   old man   ship

  a An .... brings Sir Galahad to the Round Table.

  b Sir Lancelot is Galahad's ....

  c King Arthur knows that he will not see some of his ....
  again.

  d After many years, Galahad finds the Grail on a ....

  e Galahad builds a .... for the Grail and then he dies.

25 Write the places in the sentences.

  a Arthur and Sir Gawain want to fight Sir Lancelot in ....

  b Guinevere runs away to ....

  c There is a great fight between Arthur and Mordred in ....

  d Gawain dies in ....

After you read

26 Answer these questions.

    a Something happens when Arthur is talking to Mordred. It starts Arthur's last fight. What happens?

    b Sir Bedivere doesn't throw Excalibur into the lake the first time. How does King Arthur know this?

    c Where does King Arthur die?

27 You are making a film of these stories. Who will play King Arthur, Merlin, Guinevere, Morgan le Fay and the Knights of the Round Table? Where will you film it? Why? Talk to other students.

Writing

28 You are Merlin. How did you help Arthur when he was a baby? How did you help him when he was a boy? Write about it.

29 King Arthur sometimes makes mistakes. Find three. Write one or two sentences about each mistake.

30 You are Guinevere, Queen Annoure, Morgan le Fay or the Lady of the Lake. Write about your feelings for Arthur.

31 You are Tristram. Write a letter to Isolt. You love her, but she has to marry King Mark. Tell her why.

32 You are King Arthur. Merlin is dead. Why did you love him? Why was he an important person? Write about him.

33 At the end of the book, King Arthur says he will come again. He will come when his country asks for him. Do you want him in your country now? Why (not)? Write your ideas.

34 You live in Camelot and Arthur was your king. Now he is dead. Was he a good or a bad king? Write about him.

35 Close the book. How many Knights of the Round Table can you remember? Write the names and some notes about each knight.

Answers for the Activities in this book are available from the Penguin Readers website. A free Activity Worksheet is also available from the website. Activity Worksheets are part of the Penguin Teacher Support Programme, which also includes Progress Tests and Graded Reader Guidelines. For more information, please visit: www.penguinreaders.com.

WORD LIST *with example sentences*

archbishop (n) The *Archbishop* of Canterbury has the most important job in the Church of England.

brave (adj) The child was very *brave* – he didn't cry.

castle (n) Windsor *Castle* is one of the homes of Elizabeth II and her family.

cave (n) The animals live in cold, dark *caves*.

evil (adj) He is an *evil* man and everybody hates him.

gold (adj) *Gold* watches are beautiful, but very expensive.

harp (n) The *harp* makes a beautiful sound, but not many people play it now.

helmet (n) Put your *helmets* on! The fight is going to start.

king (n) Please stand up before the *king* comes into the room.

knight (n) The *knights* climbed onto their horses and began to fight.

lady (n) The *ladies* play cards here on Tuesdays.
Margaret Thatcher was *Lady* Thatcher after she left her job.

lake (n) Let's swim across the *lake*.

magic (n/adj) When you eat the cake, you are suddenly very, very tall. It's *magic*!

nun (n) My sister is a *nun*, so of course she never married.

poison (n) He died after he drank *poison*.

queen (n) Elizabeth II is the *Queen* of England, Wales, Scotland and Northern Ireland.

scabbard (n) Take your sword out of its *scabbard* and fight!

stone (n/adj) Do you build houses from wood or *stone*?

sword (n) They fought with *swords*, and the loser died.

wound (n/v) He died from a large *wound* on his leg.

Treasure Island
Robert Louis Stevenson

A young boy, Jim Hawkins, lives quietly by the sea with his mother and father. One day, Billy Bones comes to live with them and from that day everything is different. Jim meets Long John Silver, a man with one leg, and Jim and Long John Silver go far across the sea in a ship called the *Hispaniola* to Treasure Island.

The Mummy

"Imhotep is half-dead and will be half-dead for all time."

The Mummy is an exciting movie. Imhotep dies in Ancient Egypt. 3,700 years later Rick O'Connell finds him. Imhotep is very dangerous. Can O'Connell send him back to the dead? *Based on the successful film.*

The Last of the Mohicans
James Fenimore Cooper

Uncas is the last of the Mohican Indians. He is with his father and Hawkeye when they meet Heyward. Heyward is taking the two young daughters of a British colonel to their father. But a Huron Indian who hates the British is near. Will the girls see their father again?

There are hundreds of Penguin Readers to choose from – world classics, film adaptations, modern-day crime and adventure, short stories, biographies, American classics, non-fiction, plays ...

For a complete list of all Penguin Readers titles, please contact your local Pearson Longman office or visit our website.

www.penguinreaders.com

Pirates of the Caribbean
The Curse of the Black Pearl

Elizabeth lives on a Caribbean island, a very dangerous place. A young blacksmith is interested in her, but pirates are interested too. Where do the pirates come from and what do they want? Is there really a curse on their ship? And why can't they enjoy their gold?

Matilda
Roald Dahl

When the headmistress attacks her, Matilda finds out she has extraordinary powers to protect herself. Now she isn't frightened of anyone! *Also a film starring Danny De Vito.*

Robinson Crusoe
Daniel Defoe

Robinson Crusoe is shipwrecked onto an island after a storm at sea. Are there other people? How will he survive? Will he be rescued? *A classic tale of survival based on a true story.*

There are hundreds of Penguin Readers to choose from – world classics, film adaptations, modern-day crime and adventure, short stories, biographies, American classics, non-fiction, plays ...

For a complete list of all Penguin Readers titles, please contact your local Pearson Longman office or visit our website.

www.penguinreaders.com

Longman Dictionaries

Express yourself with confidence!

---

*Longman has led the way in ELT dictionaries since 1935.
We constantly talk to students and teachers around the
world to find out what they need from a learner's dictionary.*

Why choose a Longman dictionary?

Easy to understand

Longman invented the Defining Vocabulary – 2000 of the most
common words which are used to write the definitions in our
dictionaries. So Longman definitions are always clear and easy
to understand.

Real, natural English

All Longman dictionaries contain natural examples taken from
real-life that help explain the meaning of a word and show you
how to use it in context.

Avoid common mistakes

Longman dictionaries are written specially for learners, and we
make sure that you get all the help you need to avoid common
mistakes. We analyse typical learners' mistakes and include
notes on how to avoid them.

Innovative CD-ROMs

Longman are leaders in dictionary CD-ROM innovation. Did
you know that a dictionary CD-ROM includes features to help
improve your pronunciation, help you practice for exams and
improve your writing skills?

**For details of all Longman dictionaries, and to choose
the one that's right for you, visit our website:**

www.longman.com/dictionaries